Original title:
Smoky Asks Beneath the Mermaid Dock

Author: Kätriin Kaldaru
ISBN HARDBACK: 978-1-80562-767-8
ISBN PAPERBACK: 978-1-80564-288-6

Beneath the Shimmering Depths

Beneath the waves, where secrets dwell,
The coral crowns in silence swell.
Echoes of dreams in the ocean's sweep,
Cradled softly, the world asleep.

Whispers of tides tell ancient tales,
Of moonlit nights and stormy gales.
In the deep blue, shadows glide,
Nature's dance, a mystic ride.

Fishes glitter like stars in flight,
Flitting through depths, a wondrous sight.
Amongst the ruins of ships long lost,
The treasures gleam, what a heavy cost.

Anemones wave, an elegant sway,
Luring the lost who drift astray.
In a kingdom where time drifts slow,
Beneath the shimmer, wonders grow.

The sea sings soft, a lullaby sweet,
To soothe the heart, a rhythmic beat.
For those who seek what lies below,
Will find the magic, the ebb and flow.

Tales of the Undersea World

In the depths of blue, stories unfold,
Of daring quests and treasures untold.
Mermaids whisper in voices so clear,
Inviting the brave to draw ever near.

The shipwrecks lie like giants asleep,
Guardians of secrets that the oceans keep.
Barnacles cling to their weathered dreams,
Where sunlight dances and starlight beams.

Octopuses waltz with grace and finesse,
In hidden caves, they weave and impress.
Tales spun in currents, beguiling and bright,
Reveal the wonders of day and night.

Dolphins engage in playful delight,
Their laughter bubbles like stars in the night.
As fish weave patterns in vibrant array,
Celebrate life in this watery ballet.

With every swell of the ocean's song,
The tales of the deep will carry you along.
Listen closely, let your spirit roam,
In the undersea world, you find your home.

Lanterns of the Forgotten Harbor

In the harbor deep, where fog lingers long,
Lanterns whisper, their flickers are strong.
Memory sways on the rippling tide,
As stories of sailors in shadows abide.

Once they set forth on a quest for fame,
With gold and glory at the heart of their aim.
Now the lanterns, like ghosts, softly hum,
The echo of laughter, the beat of the drum.

Each beam tells a tale of joy and despair,
Of promises made and lost to the air.
As dusk falls gently, the waters reflect,
The memories held in the souls they protect.

Seagulls cry out a mournful refrain,
Speaking of dreams that linger in vain.
With every ripple, the past comes alive,
In this forgotten harbor where shadows thrive.

So heed the call of the lanterns aglow,
For in their light, the lost stories flow.
To those seeking answers from days gone by,
The forgotten harbor will never say goodbye.

A Merfolk's Serenade

When the moon graces the deep with her light,
A merfolk's song drifts into the night.
With silvery scales and hearts full of grace,
They serenade stars in this timeless space.

Notes weave through the current, soft and bright,
Echoes of dreams that take flight.
With laughter that dances on waves so free,
They call to the sailors lost at sea.

Their melodies swirl like the tide's gentle sway,
Binding the night to the break of day.
Teaching the stars how to twinkle and gleam,
In the rhythm of waves, they find their dream.

Whispers of longing float through the blue,
As the ocean embraces each song, deep and true.
With every verse, the waters take heed,
For a merfolk's heart thrives on love's good deed.

So listen closely when the night draws near,
For the song of the sea brings joy and cheer.
In the depths of the ocean's tender embrace,
A merfolk's serenade finds its place.

Shadows on the Coral Path

Shadows dance along the reef,
Whispered secrets of the deep.
Coral castles stand in grace,
Guardians of a hidden place.

Glistening tendrils reach for light,
In the hush of deepening night.
Fish weave tales in colors bright,
Echoes of the day take flight.

A sea turtle glides with ease,
Carving paths through ocean breeze.
Songs of waves, both high and low,
In gentle swirls, they come and go.

Beneath the moon's soft, watchful gaze,
Coral whispers through the haze.
Dancing shadows, silent lore,
In a world of myth and more.

The waters' secrets never fade,
In twilight's glow, dreams are made.
Once the sun begins to rise,
Shadows wane, but hope defies.

Beneath the Glistening Surface

Beneath the waves, a realm unfolds,
Echoes of the tales untold.
Where sunbeams paint the ocean floor,
And hidden treasures wait for more.

Darting fish in hues so bright,
Sway and shimmer in the light.
Anemones in quiet sway,
Invite the curious to stay.

Octopuses weave clever dreams,
In underwater, silvery streams.
Seahorses twirl in graceful waltz,
Nature's beauty never faults.

A whisper floats on the cool tide,
Beneath the surface, secrets hide.
Life unfolds in vibrant swirls,
As ocean magic softly curls.

Forever cradled by the blue,
A haven rich with every hue.
Discovering, we learn to see,
The wondrous depths, where hearts roam free.

Murmurs of the Ocean's Heart

In the silence, whispers flow,
Murmurs soft like falling snow.
The ocean's heart, its secrets dear,
Beats with stories, crystal clear.

Waves carry tales from far and wide,
Of ships that sailed, and dreams that died.
Life beneath the beckoning sky,
Breathes in rhythm, never shy.

Whales sing songs of ancient lore,
Echoing through the ocean's core.
Starfish bask on sunlit rocks,
Time's embrace, in gentle shocks.

Bubbles rise like fleeting thoughts,
In currents where the darkness blots.
Each ripple a history unfurled,
In the canvas of the world.

The tide pulls at the moon so bright,
Binding night to morning light.
In the stillness, hearts take flight,
To dream of oceans, pure delight.

Diary of a Sunken Vessel

Beneath the waves, a ship lies low,
Wrapped in tales only the deep can know.
Its creaking bones and weathered sails,
Guard the whispers of olden trails.

Rusty anchor holds the past,
In the silence, shadows cast.
Secrets buried in salty gloom,
Life woven through the impending doom.

Barnacles cling like memories dear,
To timbers that once faced no fear.
Each plank a story, a time unspooled,
In the ocean's depths, fate is ruled.

Waves of time wash over the wreck,
Nature's canvas, history's tech.
A mermaid's song drifts through the sea,
In harmony, souls seek to be free.

Yet, in this watery grave, a spark,
A hint of light in the gathering dark.
For every end, there is a new start,
The diary lives in the ocean's heart.

The Enigma of the Coral Grove

In shadows deep where wonders dwell,
The coral whispers secrets swell.
Beneath the waves, a tale unfolds,
Of timeless dreams and treasures bold.

A dance of light, a beckoning call,
To haunting depths where legends sprawl.
Colors shimmer, a vibrant embrace,
In silence, find a tranquil space.

Curious hearts drift, drawn near,
By mysteries that call so clear.
Among the reefs, the stories weave,
A tapestry of what we believe.

With every breath, the ocean sighs,
In harmony, where the mystery lies.
Beneath the surface, life ignites,
Orchids bloom in deepest nights.

So find the grove, that secret place,
Where the sea's heartbeat sets the pace.
An enigma wrapped in azure skies,
Where coral dreams and magic rise.

A Symphony of Sea Spirits

The ocean sings a haunting tune,
As waves create a rhythmic swoon.
Sea spirits dance in twilight glow,
In harmony where soft winds blow.

With every rise, the tides confess,
Their secrets wrapped in sweet finesse.
A symphony of life takes flight,
In waters deep, where stars ignite.

Listen close to whispers light,
Each note a glimpse of pure delight.
The sea, a deep, a vast expanse,
Where mirrored worlds engage in dance.

Glistening scales in sunlit streams,
Dance to the pulse of ancient dreams.
In realms unseen, they weave and swirl,
A magic woven, a twinkling pearl.

So close your eyes and feel the sound,
Where sea and spirit twine around.
In every wave, in every sigh,
A symphony that never dies.

Beneath the Weeping Waves

Beneath the waves, the lost ones dwell,
In shadows deep, their stories swell.
The memories of time long past,
In depths where silence holds them fast.

A weeping tide, a gentle kiss,
Hides all the sorrows, all the bliss.
The current flows with tales untold,
In every ripple, hearts unfold.

Ghostly echoes, a haunting grace,
In every wave, a familiar face.
And with each crash upon the shore,
Lost souls will linger, forevermore.

Beneath the blue, the dreams reside,
In currents swirling, they must hide.
A keeper's watch in twilight's glow,
Where life and legend ebb and flow.

So let the waves their secrets speak,
In whispered tones, their comfort seek.
For in the depths, the past will weave,
The fabric of all hearts that grieve.

Revelations of the Nautical Night

In the stillness of the starry sea,
Wonders bloom like mystery.
The moonlight dances on the tide,
While shadowed whispers drift and glide.

Sailing forth on dreams of old,
With stories wrapped in silver fold.
The night unveils a cloak of truth,
In the lore of the ageless youth.

A lighthouse stands, its beacon bright,
Guiding hearts through the murky night.
The ocean's pulse, a gentle guide,
Where secrets lie and hopes confide.

In the depths of dark, a treasure glows,
A whispered tale the wind bestows.
With every wave, a new refrain,
Nautical tales through joy and pain.

So sail away on those midnight streams,
To whispered shores of silver dreams.
In the nautical night, find your way,
To revelations the stars convey.

Love Letters to a Glistening Abyss

In shadows deep, where whispers dwell,
A heart spills ink, secrets to tell.
Beneath the waves, emotions gleam,
A silent bond, a shared dream.

With every tide that ebbs and flows,
I pen my thoughts, where longing grows.
To love the depths, to fear the fall,
An endless dance, I heed the call.

As waters churn, my spirit sways,
A tender touch in moonlit rays.
Unraveled hearts, like seashells spun,
Together lost, but never done.

The currents pull, a beckoning wail,
With every note, I weave a tale.
A glistening abyss, so vast, so wide,
In liquid dreams, our souls collide.

So cast your line, and feel the pull,
In heart of oceans, ever full.
Love letters float on salty air,
Two souls united, a timeless pair.

Dreams Drifted in Saltwater Breezes

On crested waves where sunlight gleams,
I'll trace my hopes, in whispered dreams.
Each breeze that stirs, a gentle call,
To leave my fears, to rise, to fall.

With every gust, I sail away,
To distant shores where spirits play.
The salty air, a fragrant blend,
Where time stands still, and hearts transcend.

Each grain of sand, a memory spun,
Of laughter shared, adventures won.
In twilight's glow, I close my eyes,
And drift beneath these endless skies.

The moon above in silvered grace,
A guiding light, a warm embrace.
With tides that pull, and tides that push,
I find my peace, where dreams are hush.

When morning breaks, and dawn alights,
I'll cherish dreams of starry nights.
In saltwater breezes, I'll remain,
Forever free, in love's sweet reign.

The Mermaid's Lament on Wooden Planks

Upon the shore, where memories sleep,
A mermaid sings her song so deep.
With longing rife, she weeps for home,
The ocean's heart, where spirits roam.

Her voice, a symphony of sighs,
Calls to the waves, beneath the skies.
On wooden planks, she weaves her fate,
A tale of love, a heart's debate.

The salty breeze, it wraps around,
A bittersweet, enchanting sound.
With every note, a dream distills,
Of ocean depths and moonlit thrills.

Oh, how she longs for briny sea,
The cool embrace that sets her free.
But on the shore, she finds her pain,
A dance with stars, a world in vain.

Yet still she sings, through joy and sorrow,
A promise held to greet tomorrow.
With each lament on wooden planks,
A mermaid's heart forever thanks.

Currents Carry Memories Untold

In swirling tides where shadows play,
Currents guide the dreams away.
What once was near, now floats afar,
Captured still, like a drifting star.

The echoes sound from depths below,
Stories whispered, secrets flow.
Every wave a tale unfolds,
Of love lost deep, of hopes retold.

Resilient hearts, they rise and fall,
Bound by the sea's familiar call.
Embrace the depths, embrace the rise,
In ocean's heart, true solace lies.

For every memory that ebbs away,
A new dawn brings another day.
In gentle swells, our laughter dwells,
Currents carry, yet never quell.

So drift with me on waters wide,
In currents strong, we'll turn the tide.
Together we'll craft our tales untold,
In the arms of dreams, forever bold.

The Shade of the Old Shipwreck

In the shadows where whispers dwell,
A shipwreck sighs its ancient tale.
Wooden bones in silence swell,
Tales of storms, and sails that sail.

Beneath the waves, secrets hide,
Coral cloaks the sunken pride.
Fishes dart, like ghosts abide,
In the depths, where dreams confide.

Moonlight dances on the crest,
Carrying whispers from the west.
The sea's embrace, a gentle rest,
In the wreck's arms, time is blessed.

Mermaids' laughter, faint yet clear,
Calls from depths, both far and near.
Hearts of mariners, held so dear,
In the ship's guard, forever here.

Once a ship, now a memory's song,
In ocean's cradle, where it belongs.
The past and present, an unbroken throng,
In the shade where the shipwrecks strong.

A Mysterious Harbor's Invitation

The harbor waits, with secrets deep,
Inviting all who dare to leap.
Shadows dance where waters keep,
Echoes of dreams that softly weep.

Boats bob gently, kissed by night,
Strangers gather in fading light.
Waves carry tales of an unseen flight,
Mystic shores that feel just right.

Stars above, a guiding thread,
Leading souls where few have tread.
A promise lingers, softly said,
In the harbor's heart, fears are shed.

Catch the glimmer, the daring dare,
With every breath of salty air.
As whispers linger, bold and rare,
An invitation waits for those who care.

Ahoy the heart, to worlds unknown,
Where kindred spirits are gently grown.
In this harbor, a love is shown,
An endless journey, never alone.

The Jewelry of the Ocean Bed

Beneath the waves, a treasure gleams,
With pearls and shells, the ocean dreams.
Secrets wrapped in liquid beams,
The jewelry of its silent themes.

Glistening shards of coral bright,
Glowing softly, a wondrous sight.
In every stone, a story's light,
Of journeys lost in the depth of night.

Fishermen honor the ocean's deed,
As gentle currents plant the seed.
Nature's bounty is what we need,
From sapphire depths, our hearts are freed.

Each glitter tells of love and lore,
Of whispered breezes on a distant shore.
A history carved, forever more,
In treasures deep, where dreams implore.

So dive beneath the azure sprawl,
To find the gems that nature's call.
For in the depths, we hear it all,
The jewelry of the ocean's thrall.

Tales Whispers Beneath the Dock

In shadows deep where darkness dwells,
A story hums like whispered spells,
Old timbers creak with secrets near,
As fanciful tales drift upon the beer.

The river sings of days long past,
Of sailors brave and storms that cast,
Their dreams in nets, a salty breeze,
Echoes linger beneath the trees.

With lanterns bright, we gather round,
To spin the yarns where magic's found,
The laughter mingles with the night,
While stars above, they wink with light.

Each wave a tale, each splash a song,
A tapestry of right and wrong,
The moonlit path, a guiding grace,
Beneath the dock, time slows its pace.

Yet come the dawn, it all must fade,
As waking dreams in sunlight wade,
But memory holds the magic's key,
For whispered tales are meant to be.

Siren's Dreams in the Marine Twilight

In twilight's glow where waters gleam,
The siren sings of gentle dreams,
Her voice like silken threads entwined,
In every heart, her magic finds.

With shimmering scales in moonlit dance,
She weaves a spell of sweet romance,
Each ripple carries her soft call,
A melody that enchants all.

Atop the waves, the stars align,
A cosmic map, a love divine,
The ocean sighs beneath her sway,
As shadows mingle with the day.

Yet hearts must heed the tides' refrain,
For dreams may linger but can wane,
As dawn approaches with golden hue,
The siren fades from view anew.

But whispered legends linger still,
In every heart, a freshened thrill,
For though she swims beyond our sight,
Her spirit breathes in day and night.

Hushed Conversations with the Deep Blue Sea

In quiet depth where mysteries sleep,
The sea confides in whispers deep,
Her gentle sighs, a calming tune,
Beneath the silver watchful moon.

Shells cradle stories, old and wise,
Of mariners lost and hidden skies,
In ebb and flow, the secrets play,
In hushed tones that drift away.

A heart can listen, a soul can feel,
The ocean's truth, the tides that heal,
With salty breeze and tales so grand,
We dance upon the shifting sand.

In the cradle of the waves so wide,
We find our fears, our hopes can glide,
For in the depths, our dreams reside,
A voyage shared, a wondrous ride.

So let the currents guide you near,
Embrace the whispers, hold them dear,
For every wave that kisses shore,
Is life's sweet song, forevermore.

Enchanted Mists of the Harbor's Heart

Through swirling mists, the harbor glows,
Where dreams afloat like secrets flow,
Each ship a whisper, each mast a sigh,
In windswept tales that never die.

With twilight's brush, the colors blend,
Where water meets the sky's deep end,
The lanterns twinkle, a dance of light,
Embracing shadows of the night.

In every ripple, a story sings,
Of fairies, ships, and magical things,
The harbor's heart, a timeless place,
Where love and wonder find their grace.

As mist unfolds, new journeys start,
In every whisper lies a heart,
So breathe the magic, savor the view,
For the harbor's heart beats just for you.

In enchanted moments, dreams take flight,
As sailors bid farewell to night,
A promise lies in morning's hue,
That every harbor waits for you.

A Dance with Tides and Treasures

Beneath the moon's soft glow, they sway,
Whispers of secrets lost in play.
The waves embrace with gentle grace,
Urging dreams to find their place.

Amidst the currents, treasures gleam,
Glistening bright like a waking dream.
Shells, and silver, fragments of old,
Stories of sailors brave and bold.

In the rhythm of the sea's soft song,
Hearts enchanted, where we belong.
Mysterious depths hold tales untold,
Passages daring, adventures bold.

The tides bring longing, ebbing and flow,
Carried by whispers no more than a glow.
With every wave, a promise floats,
A dance recalling forgotten boats.

So let the moonlight guide your way,
In the harbor where dreams drift and sway.
For in the depths, both near and far,
Treasures await, beneath each star.

Forbidden Tales from the Harbor's Edge

In shadows cast by the fading light,
Lies a harbor that whispers of fright.
Legends tragic, wrapped in mist,
Forbidden secrets that can't be kissed.

Old mariners tell of fabled lore,
Voices tremble, hearts want more.
Of spirits haunting, lost at sea,
Echoes of past that dare to be free.

The waters churn with unshed tears,
Bearing the weight of lingering fears.
Each wave a story, each storm a sigh,
Promises made, but none to tie.

A lighthouse stands, its beam a guide,
Yet draws the wanderers to the tide.
With bated breath, they heed the call,
The harbor's edge is their final fall.

Still in the hush, when night does creep,
The tales of old beckon from sleep.
As sailors wander, they'll always find,
The harbor's secrets are intertwined.

The Lure of Waterlogged Wonders

In murky depths where shadows creep,
Ancient vessels lie in sleep.
Time's embrace has turned them gray,
Waterlogged wonders, here they'll stay.

Barnacles cling to every side,
Whispers of journeys long denied.
Adventurous hearts, drawn to explore,
Unearth the mysteries held in the shore.

Glimmers of gold in sunbeams dance,
Calling the brave to take a chance.
With nets of hope, they cast and weave,
Finding treasures that hearts believe.

As tides pull back, the wonders glow,
Alive with secrets from long ago.
Each twinkle tells of dreams once shared,
Of sailors bold, forever ensnared.

So heed the call of the water's sway,
Let curiosity guide the way.
For in every ripple, there's still a chance,
To discover life's grand, hidden dance.

Requiem for a Lost Aquatic Realm

Once vibrant waves did cradle life,
A kingdom sprawled, untouched by strife.
Corals bright and fish that play,
Now mere echoes, drifted away.

Where laughter rang in currents clear,
Now silence reigns, we shed a tear.
Oceans deep with stories to share,
All now lost in a vivid despair.

The tides recede with heavy hearts,
Reflecting dreams that deep time imparts.
Each grain of sand, a memory gone,
A requiem for the reefs we've drawn.

Yet whispers linger in the sea's embrace,
Reminding us of that sacred space.
In our hands lies the fate we hold,
To cherish and guard what once was bold.

So let us vow by moonlit swell,
To heal the waters, let our hearts swell.
For every wave that kisses the shore,
Is a chance to restore what we adore.

The Glow of Submerged Tales

In the depths where secrets lie,
Whispers dance, as shadows sigh.
Tales of old in silent gleam,
Beneath the waves, a timeless dream.

Cradled by the ocean's breath,
Stories linger, teetering on death.
Echoes of love, loss, and fate,
Merge with tides, and celebrate.

Glimmers of treasure, hidden deep,
In currents where the mermaids weep.
A lighthouse flickers, guiding light,
Through murky depths of endless night.

Mysterious sirens call to thee,
In liquid realms, wild and free.
History beneath the foam,
Awaits all those who dare to roam.

So dive with courage, find your way,
Let the enchanted waters play.
For in the glow of tales submerged,
Life and magic are gently merged.

An Odyssey of Ocean Whispers

Upon the cresting waves they soar,
Adventurers seeking distant shore.
In the breeze, a soft refrain,
Whispers of the ocean's gain.

Seagulls cry, a call to roam,
Far from hearth, and far from home.
The salt, the air, a song divine,
Lead the heart through paths entwined.

Nights beneath the endless sky,
Stars above as dreams float by.
Charting course with every breath,
An odyssey beyond all death.

With every splash, the spirit soars,
To distant lands and hidden doors.
Hope glimmers like the morning dew,
As ocean whispers guide the crew.

So sail, brave soul, on waves of fate,
Chasing the night, never too late.
For in the sea's soft, whispered calls,
Adventure waits, as courage falls.

Shadows of the Harbor's Prayer

In the harbor, shadows dance,
Woven tales of fate and chance.
Ropes and nets like dreams unfurl,
In quiet depths, a secret whirl.

Lamps flicker, casting glow,
Where sailors wander, lost in woe.
Each vessel tells a tale of grace,
Reflections mirrored in the space.

The salty air enfolds the night,
A comforting shroud, a gentle light.
In each corner linger sighs,
Of hopes and loves beneath the skies.

Midst distant echoes, hearts confide,
In shadows where the past resides.
They whisper prayers, both brave and bold,
For stories waiting to be told.

So listen close, and heed the plea,
Of the harbor, vast and free.
For in its shadows, life takes flight,
Guided by the softest light.

Fathoms of Forgotten Echoes

In ocean depths, where echoes dwell,
Forgotten whispers weave their spell.
Through layers of forgotten time,
Memories swim, a quiet rhyme.

Beneath the swell, in darkened grace,
Fathoms hold each timeworn face.
Silent tales of yesteryear,
Drift through waters, calm yet sheer.

A shipwreck's sigh, a lover's cry,
In currents where the shadows lie.
Each wave carries a tale untold,
In depths where hearts of sailors bold.

So dive beneath the sapphire hue,
Where echoes linger, old yet new.
Discover legends lost to sight,
In fathoms deep, beyond the light.

Amidst the silence, hear the call,
Of whispers hidden beneath it all.
For in those depths, your heart may find,
The echoes linger, intertwined.

Whispers of the Forgotten Brine

In the depths where shadows play,
Secrets murmur night and day.
With a sigh, the currents weave,
Tales of those who dare believe.

Oceans hold their ancient songs,
Echoes of the lost and wronged.
With a flick of silver scales,
Memory within the gales.

Ghostly ships in haunted dreams,
Sail on whispers, ride the streams.
Forgotten mariners take flight,
Chasing stars in endless night.

Softly lapping at the shore,
Echoes begging evermore.
With each wave, a story told,
Of brave hearts and treasures bold.

In the brine, their voices blend,
A symphony that has no end.
Whispers dance in frothy foam,
Each ripple calls the sea their home.

Secrets of the Saltwater Depths

With the tide, the secrets flow,
In the deep where no light glows.
Creatures dwell in shadows deep,
Guarding wonders they must keep.

Coral castles, bright and proud,
Stand in silence, shrouded, bowed.
In the silence, stories stir,
Waiting for a voice to purr.

Bubbles rise like whispered dreams,
Carried forth on silver beams.
Lost sailors linger near the sand,
Yearning for a helping hand.

Hidden treasures lie in wait,
Among the tides, they tempt fate.
Salted secrets, time's embrace,
Legacy of the ocean's grace.

What lies past the shimmering veil?
Shades of wonder, hopes to sail.
Beneath the waves, the stories strum,
Of lives entwined and battles won.

Echoes of Sunlit Waves

Beneath the sun, the waters gleam,
Laughter rolls like whispers' dream.
Gentle waves caress the shore,
Carrying tales of evermore.

Rippling laughter, soft and shy,
Plays with the clouds that wander by.
Each crest a joy, each trough a sigh,
Holding memories, high and dry.

Seagulls dance on salted air,
Chasing echoes without care.
In their flight, the stories rise,
Painting dreams in endless skies.

Sunset kisses waves of gold,
Turning hearts as night unfolds.
Twilight paints the water bright,
Softly cradling fading light.

With each swell, a promise glows,
In the depths, the love still flows.
Echoes linger in the spray,
Whispers of a brighter day.

The Twilight Tide's Lament

As the sun dips low and fades,
The twilight tide begins cascades.
Gentle murmurs weave through night,
Echoes of lost dreams take flight.

Stars awaken in the dark,
Citing tales with silver spark.
Each wave a sigh, a yearning plea,
For the past that cannot be.

The moon descends with solemn grace,
Lighting up the ocean's face.
Ripples dance with sorrow's tune,
Chasing shadows, lost too soon.

Whispers weave through drifting sand,
A tuneful ache that seems so grand.
In cradled arms, the ocean sways,
Hushed lament of twilight days.

As the night deepens its shroud,
Silence falls like a gentle cloud.
In the depths, the heartbeats blend,
A twilight tide that will not end.

The Fisherman's Forgotten Dream

In nets of twilight, secrets hide,
Beneath the waves where dreams reside.
A fisherman's hope, lost at sea,
Whispers of wonder, soft as the breeze.

Old tales linger, shadows dance,
Every cast holds a chance, a glance.
The moon's reflection, a guiding light,
Flickers like stars in the cool of night.

Each tide carries an ancient song,
Of tides that turn and dreams that long.
Forgotten wishes, driftwood tales,
Echoing softly through stormy gales.

With every ripple, a memory fades,
Of fish that glimmer in deep glades.
Fisherman's heart, both strong and frail,
In the silence of waters, he sets his sail.

So he waits by the shore, a gentle sigh,
With dreams of the ocean, lost to the sky.
Yet still in the depths, those wishes gleam,
A flicker of hope in the fisherman's dream.

Beneath the Calm, a Roar

Sunlit waters, tranquil, serene,
Beneath the surface, a fierce unseen.
Whispers of currents, tales untold,
Where shadows of giants brave and bold.

The lull of waves, a soft embrace,
Yet darkness gathers, a hidden place.
In the hush of dusk, a promise stirs,
A roaring tempest, as time blurs.

Life's hidden battles rage and churn,
For every calm, there's a fire's burn.
Echoes of struggle, the ocean's breath,
Life and death dance in quiet death.

Dare we delve where light won't shine?
The heart of the sea, is it yours or mine?
Beneath the calm, a secret thrall,
Waiting to rise, the storm will call.

At the edge of night, horizons meet,
The roar of the deep, a heartbeat sweet.
In whispers of waves, we find our place,
In the dance of shadows, a wild grace.

A Tango with the Tidal Spirits

In moonlit glades, the waters twirl,
Tidal spirits in a dance, a whirl.
Their laughter mingles with the night,
In shimmering waves, they take their flight.

Beneath the stars, a rhythmic flow,
A foamy ballet, with ebb and glow.
Seashell whispers and salty songs,
Guide the traveler where he belongs.

The ocean's heart beats in time, alive,
In each rolling wave, they thrive and strive.
A tango on tides, both fierce and grand,
We dance with spirits, hand in hand.

Fleeting shadows, bright and rare,
The sting of salt hangs in the air.
Each leap, a moment, an endless dream,
The currents weave their silken seam.

As dawn approaches, colors fade,
Yet echoes of dancing will never jade.
For tides may turn and spirits roam,
In the hearts of dreamers, they find their home.

Currents of Myth and Memory

In flowing streams of whispered lore,
Currents of myth carve out the shore.
Capturing dreams in the amber glow,
Of timeless tales where memories flow.

Legends drift on the ocean's breath,
Whispers of love, of life and death.
Every shoreline tells its tale,
In sand and foam, where dreams prevail.

In the distance, a lighthouse gleams,
Casting light on our forgotten dreams.
Guiding souls through tempestuous seas,
Chasing shadows in the evening breeze.

So listen close to the waves that crash,
To the stories woven in their splash.
For every tide carries the past's embrace,
In the flow of time, we find our place.

As we sail through the echoes of yore,
On currents that whisper forever more,
In the swell of the sea, our hearts entwined,
In the depths of memory, we are defined.

Enchanted Echoes of the Deep

In the stillness, shadows play,
Whispers of ancient tides sway,
Beneath the waves, secrets hide,
Where mermaids sing, and dreams abide.

Moonlight dances on the crest,
Mapping stars upon the rest,
Each glimmer a tale to unfold,
In the deep, where wonders hold.

Coral castles rise with grace,
Guardians of a hidden place,
Time weaves threads both bright and dim,
In the ocean's fateful hymn.

With every splash, a heartbeat's drum,
The watery world begins to hum,
Echoes from the depths arise,
A serenade beneath the skies.

So dive beneath the twinkling foam,
Where spirits of the sea call home,
In enchanted realms, hearts will leap,
To discover the magic of the deep.

A Mask of Seaweed and Shell

A mask of seaweed, green and bright,
Crafted by the waves at night,
Shells adorned with stories grand,
Echoes of a mystic land.

With ocean's breath, they rise and fall,
In secret chambers, hearkening call,
Each grain of sand tells a tale,
Of sailors lost and winds that wail.

Upon the rocks, the tide will weave,
A tapestry for those who believe,
In dreams spun by a salt-sweet breeze,
Where time dances with the seas.

A glimpse into the heart so pure,
Beneath the waves, where spirits stir,
With every ripple, a truth unfurls,
In the wonder of underwater worlds.

So wear this mask and dive so deep,
Into the waters' timeless sweep,
For in this realm, you're never alone,
Among the currents, you've found your home.

The Haunting of the Old Dock

The old dock creaks with stories lost,
Of mariners who paid the cost,
Ghostly figures roam the shore,
Seeking tales from long before.

In misty nights, the lantern glows,
Whispering secrets that it knows,
Echoes of laughter, sorrow's call,
A haunting melody for all.

Wooden planks tell of weary feet,
Bound for journeys, bittersweet,
As shadows stretch and fade away,
In memories where they long to stay.

The tide rolls in with tales of yore,
Secrets held on ocean's floor,
And in the breeze, a soft lament,
For souls whose time was never spent.

So linger by the dock so old,
Listen to the winds retold,
For in the silence of the night,
The past lives on, a fleeting light.

Celestial Sways of the Ocean

The ocean sways like gentle dreams,
Underneath the night it gleams,
Stars reflected in the tide,
Celestial dances, side by side.

As waves embrace the sandy shore,
They sing of legends, myths of yore,
A lullaby of cosmic grace,
In this vast and endless space.

The moon, a guardian, watches o'er,
Guiding ships to distant shore,
With each crest, a silken kiss,
In the stillness, find your bliss.

Through the darkness, magic flows,
In the heart, the ocean knows,
The universe within each wave,
In their depths, the brave will save.

So stretch your arms, embrace the sky,
As constellations drift and fly,
For in the ocean's rhythmic sway,
Find your spirit, let it stay.

A Fragment of Forgotten Lore

In shadows deep where whispers creep,
A tale of yore begins to seep.
Forgotten lore, in pages torn,
Awakens dreams that once were born.

The candle's light, a flickering ghost,
Reveals the truths we cherish most.
With ink of night on parchment worn,
The past emerges, twisted, shorn.

Each faded word, a silken thread,
Weaving stories of those long dead.
A traveler's map, both strange and clear,
Draws the brave and the bold near.

Old echoes call from distant shores,
With laughter, tears, and ancient roars.
Seek not just here, but inward too,
For wisdom waits in hearts so true.

So take this hint, this whispered mark,
Let curiosity light the dark.
A spark ignites the vast unknown,
In every fragment, seeds are sown.

The Riddle of the Sea Glass

On shores of dreams where ocean sighs,
The sea glass sparkles, truth in disguise.
Fragments of stories, washed from the brine,
Whispers of secrets, lost in time.

Each piece a puzzle, colors entwine,
A riddle waiting, the past speaks fine.
Emeralds gleam, and sapphires dance,
Inviting hearts to take a chance.

What tales are hidden in shards so bright?
What keepsakes linger in fading light?
As tides dictate the ebb and flow,
Seek the wisdom the waters know.

In the gentle waves, there's a voice,
Invoking dreams and daring choice.
The sea holds tales of love and loss,
Each piece a bridge, each turn a cross.

So gather the shards, let spirits rise,
In every fragment, a heart replies.
The riddle of glass, both sharp and smooth,
A magic found, a mystery's groove.

Beneath the Veil of Waves

Beneath the waves where shadows play,
A world awakens, bright as day.
A sparkling realm where dreams take flight,
In depths of blue, a dance of light.

Coral towers and fishes glide,
In currents strange, they do not hide.
Secrets murmur through the tide,
In silence wrapped, where wonders bide.

What tales does Neptune's heart conceal?
What treasures lie beneath the steel?
Echoes of laughter, the songs of yore,
Whispers of love from the ocean floor.

Ancient spirits drift and roam,
In watery halls, they find a home.
Their voices rise with the swell and foam,
Inviting the lonely to come and comb.

So dive beneath this gentle veil,
Where every surge tells a tale.
In the arms of the sea, let fears dissolve,
For mysteries wait, just waiting to solve.

Specters of the Submerged Sanctum

In the sanctum deep where echoes dwell,
The specters rise, reluctant to tell.
With watery eyes and shadowed grace,
They roam the halls of their lost place.

A tapestry of forgotten years,
Woven with laughter, stitched with tears.
Each whisper stirs the curling mist,
In flickering lights, the memories twist.

What voices call from the depths so cold?
What stories of bravery, adventures bold?
The haunted past weaves through the night,
Each heartbeat pulses with ghostly light.

Lost in the echoes of time's embrace,
The specters linger, seeking grace.
In watery dreams, their songs resound,
As they dance in shadows, forever bound.

So tread with care in the sacred gloom,
For love and loss in silence bloom.
The sanctum waits with patience grand,
Inviting those who wish to understand.

The Call of the Sea Witch

In whispers deep the waters swell,
A voice that lures from ocean's dell.
Her silver hair like moonlight streams,
A haunting song weaves in our dreams.

With tides that pull and waves that crash,
She dances near with graceful flash.
Her laughter echoes, wild and free,
The call of the beguiling sea.

Beneath the foam where shadows glide,
She guards the secrets of the tide.
In every wave, a tale confined,
Of fierce enchantments left behind.

But wary, friend, for she can twist,
A heart ignited in her mist.
For those who heed her tempting lore,
May find their souls forevermore.

So stand, if you must, on the shore,
Yet heed the sound of ocean's roar.
The sea witch waits with bated breath,
To lure away the souls of men.

Legends Beneath the Sea's Surface

In ocean depths, where legends sleep,
The whispers of the ancients creep.
With tentacles of time and fate,
Their stories spin in currents great.

From shipwrecked dreams and sailors lost,
Each heart once bold, now pays the cost.
Beneath the waves, a world unseen,
Where kings and queens of oceans glean.

Coral castles rise and fall,
Echoing with the siren's call.
Ghostly ships roam endless deep,
Guarding treasures buried deep.

With every tide that ebbs and flows,
New tales emerge, and old ones close.
In watery graves, in silence bound,
The legends wait, forever drowned.

So listen close when tempests roar,
For history's voice from ocean's floor.
The tales of old persist and thrive,
In depths where dreams and myths survive.

Currents of Timeless Lore

The sea enfolds a tapestry,
Of lore that dances wild and free.
In ancient currents, stories wade,
Of secrets lost and memories made.

With every wave, a whisper grows,
Of lovers' calls and hidden foes.
The winds of time like sirens sing,
As shadows drift on ocean's wing.

From tempest's roar to waters still,
The currents flow, the echoes fill.
In silent depths, the tales arise,
Of brave hearts bold beneath the skies.

As sailors navigate the night,
They search for stars, for guiding light.
Each journey leads to shores unknown,
Where ancient myths are ever shown.

So sail away on waters wide,
Let currents carry you and guide.
For in each tide there lies some lore,
A timeless tale forevermore.

Dreaming Beneath Aquatic Stars

In tranquil depths where dreams unfold,
The night is rich with tales retold.
Beneath the waves, the starlight beams,
Awakening our wildest dreams.

The ocean floor, a velvet sky,
Where shimmering fish like comets fly.
In every bubble, wishes rise,
As starlit waves caress our sighs.

Here magic swims in shadows cast,
Of journeys taken, futures past.
With every breath of salty air,
We dance along the ocean's care.

Wrapped in the ocean's soft embrace,
The worlds collide in timeless space.
In dreams of depths, we lose our way,
In gentle whispers, night meets day.

So rest your heart beneath the waves,
Where every soul the ocean saves.
In aquatic stars, we'll find our place,
And drift beyond in endless grace.

Beneath the Waves of Forgotten Lore

Whispers rise from shadowed depths,
Where mermaids sing of lost regrets.
The tides have tales so softly spun,
Beneath the waves, where dreams are won.

Ancient ships in silence rest,
Their stories held in ocean's chest.
In every ripple, secrets twine,
With echoes of a world divine.

Still waters wait for hearts to hear,
The melody of aged fears.
A dance of souls in waters vast,
Connecting futures with the past.

Moonlit beams on silken sands,
Guide sailors lost to promised lands.
With hope, they cast their nets of dreams,
For in the depths, all is as it seems.

Beneath the waves, beneath the swell,
A hidden magic casts its spell.
In every current, life's embrace,
A journey found, a sacred place.

The Cradle of Coral Dreams

In the cradle of the ocean deep,
Coral beds where secrets sleep.
Colors burst in vivid streams,
As mermaids weave their silent dreams.

Gentle currents hum a tune,
Beneath the watchful, glowing moon.
In this kingdom, life does sway,
A nightly dance, a bright array.

Every creature plays a part,
In coral's bloom, they leave their art.
With every wave, the tales unfold,
Of love, of courage, magic bold.

Softly swaying in the tide,
Joy and sorrow intertwined.
Through vibrant reefs, the stories flow,
Of all who wander, seek, and know.

In this cradle, dreams are spun,
Of adventures waiting to be won.
A world alive with color and cheer,
In the cradle of dreams, all is near.

Gossamer Threads between Worlds

Between the realms of sea and sky,
Gossamer threads that stretch and tie.
A weaving made of light and grace,
These filaments craft a timeless space.

In twilight's glow, the paths do blend,
Where whispers float and starlight bends.
Through every heart, these threads will weave,
A promise kept, we shall believe.

Dreamers dance on strands so fine,
With hopes that spark like fireflies shine.
In this tapestry, we find our way,
Through shadows cast into the day.

Across the edges, realms collide,
With every heartbeat, worlds abide.
In silken strands, our fates embrace,
Invisible ties that time can trace.

Listen close to the tales they tell,
Of journeys shared, both heaven and hell.
In these gossamer threads, we blend,
A sacred bond that will not end.

Beneath Driftwood and Fantasies

Beneath the driftwood, stories sigh,
Where dreams are tangled, spirits fly.
In weathered wood, the echoes dwell,
Of whispered hopes, a stirring spell.

Seagulls wheel in the golden light,
Their cries a song of pure delight.
In this sanctuary, lost and found,
Magic weaves through the living sound.

Each grain of sand, a memory holds,
The tales of love and journeys bold.
From shore to sea, from sky to ground,
In driftwood's shade, new worlds abound.

With every tide, new dreams are drawn,
Where sunlight breaks and shadows yawn.
In this haven, hearts intertwined,
In every corner, love aligned.

So linger here, let spirits roam,
For beneath driftwood, we find home.
In the embrace of fantasy's gift,
A treasure deep, our souls uplift.

Dreaming of a Currents' Embrace

In the hush of twilight's glow,
Whispers dance where breezes blow.
Waves of silver gently sway,
Cradled dreams afloat, they play.

Stars above like secrets twink,
In the depths, the fish do blink.
Ocean's heart, a tender song,
Where the souls of dreams belong.

Rippling tales beneath the tide,
Where timeless marvels coincide.
In the current's soft caress,
Lies a world where we confess.

Guided by the moon's own light,
Sailors find their dreams at night.
Through the dark, they seek the flame,
Each heart whispers a name.

Tides will pull and tides will swell,
In this realm of dreams, they dwell.
With a breath, the voyage starts,
In the depths, we share our hearts.

Haiku of the Deep Blue

Endless waves whisper,
Secrets of the deep blue sea,
Time drifts with the tide.

Stars like pearls above,
In the ocean's soft embrace,
Dreams float in silence.

Beneath the surface,
Life sleeps in shadows and rays,
Mystery and peace.

Whales sing through the night,
Melodies of ancient tales,
Guided by the stars.

In a world so vast,
Fragile moments captured still,
In the heart of blue.

A Port of Secrets

At the edge of the world,
Where whispers never fade,
Lies a port wrapped in dreams,
And shadows softly played.

Tattered sails like stories,
Drift across the starlit bay.
Each vessel holds a secret,
Of long-forgotten days.

Figures in the twilight,
Trade their glances and tales,
In the flicker of lanterns,
Sails unfurl like veils.

Beneath the hidden starlight,
Lies a map both wise and old,
Each line a whispered breath,
Of adventures yet untold.

In this port of wonder,
Every heart can find its song,
Where the past meets the present,
And we all belong.

Mists of the Forgotten Shore

On the edge of twilight's breath,
Misty veils begin to form,
Shadows weave through whispers soft,
In the night, the sea lies warm.

Dreamers tread on silken sands,
Where the ocean's sighs are found,
Each step echoes mysteries,
Lost within the murmured sound.

Ghostly ships pass through the fog,
With tales forever muffled,
In the embrace of what once was,
Where echoes are still shuffled.

Moonlight spills in silver streams,
Guiding hearts that roam and seek,
Through the mists lies ancient lore,
In silence, the secrets speak.

Walk the path where spirits dwell,
Among the dreams that never fade,
Clothed in radiant mysteries,
The forgotten will be made.

A Silken Thread of Seafoam

In the hush of dawn's embrace,
A silken thread begins to trace,
The dance of waves, a whispered song,
Where sea and sky to dreams belong.

With every tide, the stories weave,
Of sailors lost, and those who leave,
Secrets carried on the breeze,
Faint echoes of the ocean's tease.

Upon the shore where shells reside,
The ancient tales, they lingering bide,
In silver hues, the sunbestows,
A tapestry that only grows.

So listen close, O wanderer bold,
To the sea's heart, a map of gold,
For in its depths, the world awaits,
A saga penned by fickle fates.

With echoes sweet, the waters call,
A silken thread that binds us all,
To nature's whims, to fantasy's glee,
In the depths of blue, where all are free.

Fables from the Deep Blue

Beneath the waves, where shadows play,
Fables rest, both night and day,
The kraken stirs, the mermaids sing,
In watery realms, where wonders spring.

Anemones dance with gentle grace,
They hold the dreams of every face,
Fishermen's tales of valor and woe,
Dancing like currents, to and fro.

The dolphins leap, a joyful sight,
Telling stories in the soft twilight,
Whispers carried on the tides,
Where every creature's magic hides.

The coral's hues, a vibrant spark,
They house the dreams within the dark,
In every reef, a world untold,
Of fables spun in threads of gold.

So heed the call of ocean's breath,
In every wave, there's life and death,
Fables woven in the deep blue sea,
Invite the heart to wander free.

Ripples of Ancient Stories

Around the stones where lilies grow,
Ripples form in the soft glow,
Each one whispers tales of yore,
Of mystic lands on a distant shore.

The tides recede, like breaths of fate,
Unveiling paths to contemplate,
Mermaid whispers, ghostly light,
A portal to the ancient night.

In caverns deep, the secrets hide,
Amongst the shells, the sea's good tide,
A flicker here, a shimmer there,
Echoes of lost dreams fill the air.

The moonlight weaves a silver thread,
Through waters dark, where spirits tread,
Ripples speak of loves long past,
Their timeless rhythm unsurpassed.

So dive beneath the shimm'ring waves,
And seek the life that water saves,
For in each ripple, a story lies,
A testament beneath the skies.

Secrets in the Tide Pools

Upon the rocks where water pools,
Secrets hide from prying fools,
In every curve, a treasure gleams,
The whispers of forgotten dreams.

A starfish clings, a hermit strays,
In tide's embrace, they find their ways,
Curled shells hold the ocean's sigh,
As waves of time drift slowly by.

The seaweed dances, sways with grace,
In shady nooks, they find their space,
A kingdom small, lush and profound,
Where life abounds beneath the ground.

So venture forth with watchful eyes,
For in the pools, true wonder lies,
Each secret guard, a tale to share,
Of nature's magic, bold and rare.

When daylight fades, and shadows creep,
In tide pools deep, the ocean sleeps,
With secrets stored in every crack,
The voice of sea calls us back.

Secrets of the Glimmering Abyss

In depths where shadows play and weave,
Whispers stir the silent seas,
Mysteries held, none dare believe,
Eldritch tales on evening breeze.

Glimmering sighs and shimmers bold,
Light dances through the depths of night,
Secrets shimmer, ages old,
In twilight's soft, enchanted light.

Beneath the waves where mermaids dwell,
Songs of old, a haunting tune,
In magic's grasp, all secrets swell,
Underneath the watchful moon.

Each heart that beats beneath the foam,
Holds dreams of worlds yet unexplored,
In currents deep, we find our home,
By the tales of ocean's lore.

A dance of creatures, sleek and bright,
Twisting through the ocean's song,
In enchanted waves, a pure delight,
Where every soul learns they belong.

Beneath the Echoing Waves

Beneath the waves, the stories flow,
In silent whispers, secrets glide,
With echoes deep, they ebb and grow,
While unseen wonders seek to hide.

Shadows twist through coral dream,
A realm enchanted, soft and sweet,
Where glistening pearls in moonlight gleam,
And time, in gentle rhythm, beats.

Currents churn with ancient lore,
The language of the dark and deep,
With every swell, we long for more,
And in their depths, our stories sleep.

A lullaby of waters vast,
Calls forth the brave, the kindred heart,
To dive beneath, embrace the past,
And find their place in ocean's art.

So let the tide, like dreams, arise,
With every wave, our spirits soar,
In depths beneath the starry skies,
To dance forever on the shore.

Whispers from the Aquatic Realm

From quiet depths, the echoes rise,
As secrets glide on ocean's hum,
In shimmering dark, the truth belies,
Awakening the heart to come.

In shadows where the sea sprites play,
Mystical beings weave and twirl,
With laughter light, they lead the way,
Through watery realms where dreams unfurl.

Beneath the surface, magic swells,
In every droplet, lives a tale,
An ancient force of tides and bells,
Whispers carried on the gale.

In moonlit dances, creatures glide,
The secrets shared are pure and bright,
In every wave, love's gentle tide,
Stirs the depths of starry night.

Hold fast to wonders, dare to dive,
In aquatic realms, the heart will mend,
A symphony of souls alive,
Where whispers call and never end.

Treasures in the Midnight Current

Beneath the waves, where treasures gleam,
In midnight's kiss, the secrets hide,
A treasure trove of hopes and dreams,
In every current, love's abide.

The silver fish, like stars, they shine,
As shadows weave their tales of old,
In timeless realms, the heart aligns,
With whispered truths, both brave and bold.

In depths where silence paints the scene,
A symphony of colors burst,
Where every flicker speaks of keen,
Adventures lost, yet never cursed.

So dive into the midnight sea,
With open arms, embrace the flow,
For every heart that dares to be,
Shall find the treasures they can sow.

With every tide, new dreams remerge,
In currents deep, where wonders dwell,
The midnight songs of life converge,
And in their grasp, we find our spell.

Glimmers of Hope in the Nautical Night

Beneath the stars, the shadows dance,
A whisper of dreams in the moon's embrace.
Waves carry tales of old romance,
In the stillness, a heart finds its place.

The lighthouse beams a guiding light,
Its beam a promise, steadfast and true.
Through storms that rage and darkest night,
There blooms a hope in the ocean hue.

With every crash, a song is sung,
Of sailors brave and lost at sea.
In caverns deep, where tales are spun,
Echoes of courage set spirits free.

A glimmer shines on a sailor's brow,
Igniting dreams of distant shores.
The tides may turn, but here and now,
Hope wafts gently through the ocean roars.

As dawn approaches, the darkness fades,
The sky ignites with fiery gold.
Through endless trials, hope invades,
A treasure worth more than precious gold.

The Call of the Deep: A Siren's Song

In the depths where shadows weave,
A voice emerges, sweet and clear.
It calls to sailors who dare believe,
In the haunting melody they hear.

The waves, like whispers, lap the shore,
As the siren sings a tune of woe.
With every note, they long for more,
To chase the echoes where dreams may go.

Her laughter dances on the breeze,
A symphony of desires unchained.
Through cold and depth, it aims to please,
But hearts may falter, and souls be drained.

Yet in her song lies beauty rare,
A glimpse of what the heart can hold.
For those who listen, in depths unaware,
Find magic woven in stories told.

As tides rise high, the night unfolds,
The siren's call, both cruel and sweet.
To venture forth, the brave and bold,
Must heed the rhythm, and feel the beat.

Mysteries Wrapped in Seafoam Veils

Beneath the waves, a secret stirs,
Wrapped in veils of seafoam white.
Echoes of time in gentle purrs,
Whispering softly in endless night.

Coral gardens, treasures untold,
Guarded fiercely by creatures shy.
In shadows deep, the stories unfold,
Of ancient sailors and lost sky.

Each ripple tells a tale anew,
Of mermaids dancing with finned delight.
And in the depths, the unknown grew,
Drawing the brave into its night.

The moonlit glimmers, a dance of fate,
As shadows play on the ocean floor.
What secrets hold the waves so great?
The mystic depths ever seek more.

In the twilight's glow, there lies a place,
Where dreams and fears quietly meld.
Wrapped in seafoam's soft embrace,
The heart's own yearning is gently held.

Reflections of Light on Ocean Surfaces

The sun dips low; the sky ignites,
A canvas painted in colors bright.
On ocean's face, a dance of lights,
Reflecting tales of day and night.

Ripples shimmer like fleeting dreams,
Crafted by winds that play and twist.
Each wave a whisper, or so it seems,
Telling of moments that linger and mist.

Stars emerge as shadows flee,
Their glimmers caught in twilight's weave.
The ocean's heart beats wild and free,
A rhythm that none can deceive.

In the silence, nature sings,
As dusk wraps tightly its velvet cloak.
With every tide, the magic clings,
And in stillness, the soul awoke.

So let your heart drift on the waves,
Beneath the skies where wonders thrive.
For in the ocean's depths, each saves,
A piece of light, forever alive.

The Siren's Hidden Song

In depths where silence weaves its thread,
The sirens hum, where few have tread.
With whispers soft, they call the brave,
Enticing souls beneath the wave.

Their voices blend with ocean's tune,
A melody beneath the moon.
In crashing waves, a secret lies,
A truth unveiled, in lullabies.

Beware, dear sailor, of their call,
For hearts may leap, then softly fall.
In tangled kelp and swirling foam,
The hidden song can steal your home.

Yet find their grace, and eyes may gleam,
In ocean's depths, you'll find a dream.
To dance with shadows, spirits rise,
Where time is still beneath the skies.

So listen close, and heed the tide,
For every song has magic inside.
And if you're brave and wish to roam,
Their hidden song will lead you home.

Mysteries of the Moonlit Water

Beneath the stars, the waters gleam,
A world awakens, lost in dreams.
With silver beams that paint the night,
The moon whispers tales in soft twilight.

The fish swim low, with colors bright,
As shadows dance in liquid light.
Secrets stir, in currents bold,
The mysteries of truths untold.

Each ripple holds a tale of old,
Of sailors brave and treasures gold.
In whispers soft, the nightingale,
Recites the lore of every tale.

The mermaids sing, their voices pure,
Of love and loss, their hearts endure.
In watery depths, where silence reigns,
The moonlit water holds their chains.

So sail beneath the glowing moon,
And heed the calling of the tune.
For in each wave, the night will share,
The mysteries that linger there.

Shadows of the Ocean's Murmurs

In shrouded depths where shadows play,
The ocean's whispers drift away.
With every wave a story spun,
Of evening stars and setting sun.

The depths conceal forgotten lore,
Of ancient ships and battles sore.
Their echoes rise on wistful breeze,
A melody that seeks to please.

The creatures glide, both fierce and fair,
In hidden realms, with silent flare.
Their shadows weave through darkened halls,
Where whispered secrets gently call.

The clam holds pearls, a gleaming prize,
Beneath the tide, where silence lies.
From every nook, a truth unfurls,
A tapestry of hidden worlds.

So wander deep, and seek the signs,
In ocean's heart, where mystery shines.
Embrace the shadows, let them be,
The whispers of the deep blue sea.

The Mermaid's Heartbeat

In coral caves, where stillness dwells,
The mermaid weaves her gentle spells.
With silver hair and eyes of sea,
Her heartbeat echoes wild and free.

She sings of tides and rippling waves,
Of ancient lore, of hidden graves.
Her laughter rings like crystal chimes,
Resonating through the sands of time.

Each splash of fin, a dance of grace,
In twinkling light, a fleeting trace.
Her heart, a rhythm, strong and clear,
Calls those who wander, far and near.

With every stroke beneath the swell,
A story waits, a magic spell.
In dreamy depths, love's longing stirs,
In ocean's heart, where hope occurs.

So chase the stars that hesitate,
For mermaid's song may change your fate.
And with her heartbeat, lost and found,
The ocean's love will know no bound.

Whispers of the Undersea

In the realm where shadows sleep,
Mermaids sing their secrets deep,
Bubbles dance upon the tide,
Where ancient whispers gently glide.

Coral castles bathe in light,
Guarded by the starry night,
Seahorses drift with grace and glee,
In this world, forever free.

Octopus writes with ink so bold,
Tales of treasures long foretold,
Ships that sank in storms of yore,
Lie in silence on the ocean floor.

The deep blue cradles every sigh,
From creatures low to skies up high,
With every wave, a story swells,
In the depths where magic dwells.

With currents swirling, dreams take flight,
In the undersea's soft twilight,
Listen close and you might hear,
The whispers of the world down here.

Secrets of the Shimmering Depths

In depths where sunlight fades away,
The waters weave a soft ballet,
Secrets murmur with the tide,
In hidden grottos where treasures bide.

Flickering scales and playful teeth,
Guard stories of the ocean's wreath,
At twilight's hour when shadows blend,
The sea unfolds, its tales to lend.

Glimmers dance on the ocean's face,
Echoing a forgotten place,
Oysters cradle pearls so rare,
While the seaweed whispers, unaware.

The stingrays glide in calm embrace,
Tracing paths through water's grace,
Nautilus spirals, wise and old,
Charting secrets yet untold.

A lighthouse flickers in the foam,
Guiding sailors safely home,
Yet the depths, they hold and keep,
A treasure trove of dreams to reap.

Echoes from the Tide's Embrace

In the cradle of waves' caress,
Echoes beckon, soft and press,
A lullaby from ocean's heart,
Where every tide plays its part.

Moonlit ripples dance and sway,
Carrying heartbeats far away,
The ocean speaks in gentle tones,
To the lost and weary bones.

From rocky shores to sandy bays,
The sea reveals its countless ways,
Crabs scuttle with their hidden dreams,
While silver fish swim in glistening streams.

As twilight glows, the waters sing,
Of hidden depths and wondrous things,
Anemones sway in rhythmic time,
In the ocean's tale, there's magic sublime.

So hush your thoughts, let silence breathe,
In the salty air, find your ease,
For in the tide's sweet, soft embrace,
Every soul finds its rightful place.

Shadows Beneath the Floating Quay

Beneath the quay, where shadows linger,
The secrets wave with each soft finger,
Creeking boats in the evening mist,
Whisper stories not to be missed.

Lanterns flicker, their glow reflects,
In waters deep where time connects,
Ghostly fish weave in and out,
Haunting dreams they craft about.

Barnacles clutch to wooden posts,
Echoing the sailor's boasts,
Fishers recounting thrilling tales,
While the evening breeze gently exhales.

In quiet depths where memories blend,
Rippling tides hold love to send,
The heart of the sea beats strong and true,
Dancing shadows for me and you.

Though the quay may sway and creak,
The promises of the ocean speak,
For beneath each wave and shadow's sway,
Lie the dreams of every day.

Dances in Lunar Reflections

Beneath the moonlit, silken skies,
The shadows twirl and gently rise.
With whispers soft, the night unfolds,
As secrets dance in silver golds.

In echoes bright, the stars collide,
A tapestry of dreams imbibed.
With every step, the magic hums,
As nature's song, it gently strums.

A sighing breeze, a fleeting glance,
Awake the spirit, urge the dance.
In this embrace, all time suspends,
As dance and dream, the heart transcends.

The gauzy mist begins to churn,
As shadows shift, we yearn and learn.
With every twinkling, distant flare,
The night unveils its tender care.

So let us sway beneath the light,
And lose ourselves in pure delight.
For in this world of moonlit glow,
We find the steps we long to know.

The Ghosts of Distant Shores

Upon the waves, the whispers call,
A lullaby from ancient thrall.
The ghosts of ships that sailed before,
Now linger still on distant shore.

Their echoes blend with sea's caress,
As mournful tales break through the press.
Each crashing wave, a haunting song,
Of lives and loves that drifted long.

With salt and mist entwined with tears,
A history that spans the years.
The lighthouse stands, a beacon bright,
Guiding the souls lost in the night.

In flickering light, the shadows play,
As memories glide like clouds of gray.
The vengeful storms and tranquil seas,
Conceal the heart's long-lost decrees.

So listen close to ocean's plea,
The hidden tales of you and me.
In every breeze, their whispers soar,
The ghosts shall dance forevermore.

Tides of Lost Dreams

The tide pulls back, revealing sands,
Where hopes once cast by eager hands.
Yet in the depths, they still remain,
A gentle stir, a sweet refrain.

Each ebb and flow tells stories old,
Of wishes whispered, fears retold.
The coral deep, a cradle soft,
Holds secrets where the heart takes off.

Though dreams may wash like shells aground,
They shimmer brightly, yet unbound.
With every wave that rolls anew,
A chance to start, to chase what's true.

The stars above keep watchful touch,
As currents swirl and urge us, much.
In moonlit night, our spirits gleam,
Embracing tides of lost, sweet dreams.

So let the waters guide your way,
For in their depths, the dreams shall stay.
With every wave, with every sigh,
The tides of hopes will never die.

Lullabies from the Sea Floor

At ocean's depth, the lullabies,
In liquid notes, a soft reprise.
The sea floor hums, a gentle tune,
Where shadows dance by silver moon.

With coral blooms, the whispers twirl,
As starfish sway in rhythmic whirl.
Sea turtles glide, a graceful waltz,
In tranquil dreams, they free our faults.

The echo's drift, a soothing balm,
In salty air, the world is calm.
For every song the sea imparts,
Is woven deep in longing hearts.

So close your eyes, let go of fear,
Embrace the melodies you hear.
For in this realm, where waters gleam,
We find the peace in every dream.

The tides may roll, but still they sing,
In currents soft, our souls take wing.
Lullabies call from depths untold,
In every wave, a tale unfolds.

Trials of the Nautical Traveler

Beneath the sky's vast, endless dome,
The waves like whispers, draw me home.
A tempest brews on the horizon's edge,
With courage strong, I make my pledge.

The sails unfurl, my spirit soars,
Through storms and trials, I seek the shores.
Each gust a challenge, each tide a test,
Yet in the heart's compass, I find my quest.

The stars above, they guide my way,
As moonlight dances on ocean's sway.
With salt on my lips, and wind in my hair,
I journey onward, my dreams laid bare.

From golden harbors to distant lands,
Each port a story, each grain of sands.
The whispering sea, a timeless friend,
In her embrace, all journeys blend.

In every wave, a lesson learned,
With every tide, the lanterns burned.
And so I travel, through night and day,
For in the voyage, I find my way.

The Murmur of Distant Whales

In twilight's hush, they sing their song,
The distant whales, where dreams belong.
Their voices echo through the deep,
In rhythms vast, where shadows sleep.

A lullaby from the ocean's heart,
In gentle waves, they play their part.
A world unseen, beneath the tide,
Where secrets of the sea abide.

They dance through waters, old and wise,
With stories woven, like the skies.
Each splash a page, each dive a line,
In this symphony, the stars align.

With every leap, the waters swell,
An ancient tale, they long to tell.
In currents strong, their spirits rise,
Guided by the moon's soft sighs.

Through time's embrace, they glide and roam,
In darkened depths, they find their home.
So listen close, let silence speak,
For in their murmur, the heart will seek.

Calligraphy of Tides

The tide rolls in, a script divine,
Each wave a letter, each foam a line.
With sweeping arcs, they draw the shore,
In flowing ink, forevermore.

The ocean's pen, in gentle sway,
Writes stories new with each new day.
In swirling eddies, past tales blend,
Where ocean's whispers, never end.

A dance of currents, an artful play,
As water weaves, the dawn's ballet.
With salty breath, the breeze imparts,
The language spoken by sea's old hearts.

Each grain of sand, a silent note,
In nature's song, forever wrote.
And as the currents pull and tease,
Each tidal wave builds on the breeze.

So come and watch the tides create,
The calligraphy of love and fate.
In every swell, the sea will write,
Its timeless tale by day and night.

Legends Written in Sand and Sea

Upon the shore, where stories dwell,
Legends rise, as tides can tell.
In shifting sands, the past unfolds,
Whispers of sailors and treasures bold.

With each new wave, a tale begins,
Of daring quests and fateful sins.
Their ghostly ships on waters glide,
Yet in the foam, their dreams abide.

The sun dips low, a canvas bright,
As dusk unveils the stars' soft light.
And in the depths, the echoes cling,
Of hopes ignited, of hearts that sing.

Lost treasures wait in ocean's hold,
A saga spun of riches untold.
And where the tide meets the sandy strand,
Legends thrive, as dreams expand.

So gather round, and hear the sea,
For in its depths, our history.
In every wave and whisper clear,
Lie the legends we hold dear.

The Undercurrents of Time

In shadows deep, where whispers grow,
Echoes of ages long ago.
Threads of fate in liquid weave,
Timeless secrets, who believes?

Rippling dreams on currents flow,
Memories dance, a silent show.
The past concealed beneath the waves,
An ancient song the ocean craves.

Silent clocks in depths reside,
Marking moments cast aside.
Beneath the tide, the stories blend,
A liquid realm where time can bend.

Each ripple tells of loves and losses,
Hidden trails, forgotten bosses.
With every pulse, the ages creep,
Undercurrents, dark and deep.

In whispered tones, the waters sigh,
Beneath the vast and starlit sky.
A journey vast, yet close to home,
In the arms of time, we roam.

Tales of the Drowned Mariner

Beneath the waves, a sailor sleeps,
His tales of woe the ocean keeps.
With salt-stained dreams and sunken pride,
He haunts the tides, where shadows bide.

The ship he sailed, a phantom nautilus,
Weaving through storms, so treacherous.
Echoes of laughter, now a mournful tune,
His heart lost to the tempest's moon.

A compass spun by fate's cruel hand,
No shore in sight, no promised land.
With every wave, he yearns for light,
But darkness wraps him, holding tight.

He seeks the stars, burnt out and dim,
To guide his way from ocean's whim.
Yet tangled in seaweed's embrace,
He finds his peace in this cold place.

Tales of the drowned shall never die,
Their wisdom sharp as seagull's cry.
So heed the winds when they lament,
For mariners lost, and the lives they spent.

Singing Stones of the Deep Sea

In hidden grottos, stones do hum,
Echoes of ages, softly come.
Voices weave through currents wide,
In harmony, they swell with pride.

The seashells gather, wise and old,
Each secret kept, a story told.
A chorus born of silt and clay,
Resonant notes of yesterday.

Wave after wave, the music flows,
Birth of a legend where beauty grows.
With each ebb and tide, the stones do sing,
Of love and loss and the joys they bring.

From the ocean's heart, a lullaby,
Drifting softly, it hugs the sky.
The pebbles dance under starlit charms,
Embraced in nature's tender arms.

Oh, listen close, and you shall hear,
The singing stones call ever near.
In the depths of blue, a timeless rhyme,
Their melodies weave the fabric of time.

The Enchanted Piers of Yore

Amidst the mist, where legends dwell,
Stand ancient piers, with tales to tell.
With creaking wood and salt-kissed air,
They whisper secrets, hearts laid bare.

Once bustling with laughter, bright and loud,
Now cloaked in silence, under a shroud.
Memories linger like a fading trace,
In every board, a cherished face.

Fishermen's songs rise with the tide,
While the echoes of dreams, they never hide.
Beneath the stars, they watch and yearn,
For swaying boats and lanterns' burn.

Ghostly figures drift through the night,
Dancing in shadows, lost from sight.
The piers remember, though time will flee,
With every tide, they hold the key.

So venture forth, and seek the lore,
Of enchanted piers that stand before.
For in their heart, the past is stored,
A bridge to dreams, forever adored.